THE STARTING POINT LIBRARY

| MATHS |

Seaside Maths

THE DANBURY PRESS
A Division of Grolier Enterprises, Inc.

These children are at the seashore.
They look down on the sea.
There are fish under the water.
Sea birds fly above their heads.

Shells have lovely shapes.
Some are big.
Others are small.
How many shells are stuck to the rocks?

August 2nd

Jan	Feb	Mar	Apr	May	Jun
Jul	Aug	Sep	Oct	Nov	Dec

We have holidays in the summer.
What season is it now?
How many months to the summer?

4

The carousel goes around in a circle.
Use your hands to show
how the other things move.

These creatures live in the sand and sea.
Their bodies are made up of parts.
These are called segments.
Can you count their segments?

What has made the pebbles so smooth?
Can you find pebbles
with different shapes and sizes?

The skin diver is swimming in deep water.
The children are playing
in shallow water.
Is the water in your bath deep or shallow?

8

How many men pull the boat
over the sand?
How many men move the boat
on the rollers?
Which boat is easiest to move?

How many things
fly above the children's heads?
Is the helicopter above the birds?

10

These plants and fish live in the sea.
Look at the shape of the jellyfish.
Can you find a starfish?
How many arms does it have?

This boy is paying for a donkey ride.
Other children buy ice cream and drinks.
Does a donkey ride cost more
than an ice cream?

brother mother sister father

The family try to ring the bell.
The graph shows what happens.
Can you retell the story?

13

There are many shapes on the beach.
Can you see a ball?
What shape are the flags?
How many cones can you find?

Can you find the shapes again?
Can you see a circle?
Find a triangle and a rectangle.

The fat man is being weighed.
His mass is 250 pounds.
What is your mass?

16

The children are playing on the beach.
They are filling their buckets.
Which do you think will be heavier:
a bucket of pebbles or of water?

The children cover their mother with sand.
The net covers part of the beach.
Which covers more: the net or the towel?

18

Do you think it is a hot day?
How do you know?
Is it warmer or cooler in the water?

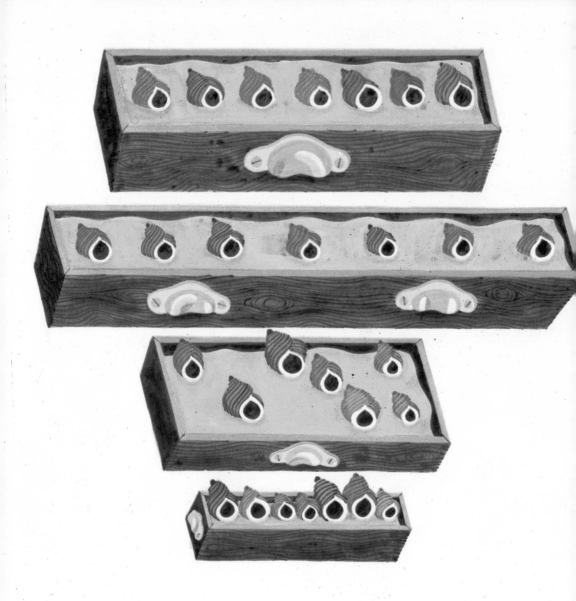

The children have collected shells.
Which box has the least number of shells?
How many shells are in each box?
How many shells altogether?

The sea makes patterns in the sand.
What is the girl doing?
Can you see her reflection?
Look at your reflection in a mirror.

Find the two boats that are moved
by the wind.
How do the children move their boat?
What moves the liner?

At high tide the water covers the beach.
Which picture shows high tide?

The children are putting things into water.
Some things float and some sink.
Can you find things which float or sink?
Make a set of things which float.

24

What time did the children
go into the pool?
When did they come out?
How long were they in the water?

25

The children are dropping balls.
The balls are bouncing.
Find the ball which bounces highest.

26

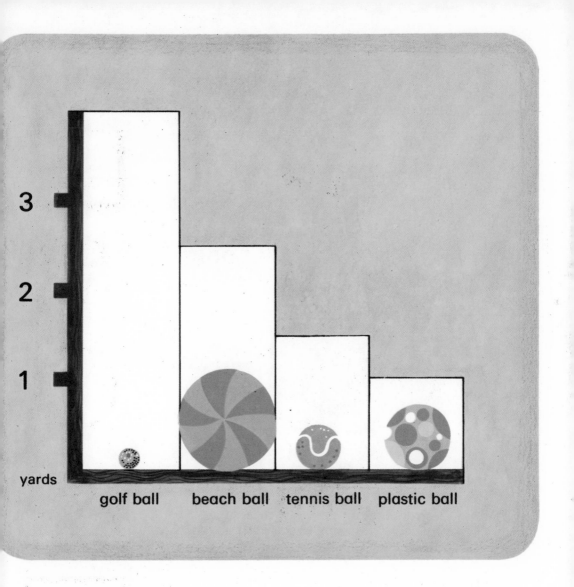

3

2

1

yards

golf ball   beach ball   tennis ball   plastic ball

This picture shows how high
the balls bounced.
How high did the tennis ball bounce?
Which ball bounced 2½ yards?

27

Index

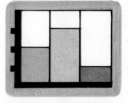